The Art of War versus The Art of Pool

How Sun Tzu would play pocket billiards

Allan P. Sand

PBIA Certified Billiards Instructor

ISBN 978-1-62505-215-5
Print 7x10

ISBN 978-1-62505-375-6
Print 6x9

ISBN 978-1-62505-537-8
eBook format

Copyright © 2009 Allan P. Sand

All rights reserved under International and Pan-American Copyright Conventions.

Published by Billiard Gods Productions.
Santa Clara, CA 95051
U.S.A.

For the latest information about books and videos, go to:
http://www.billiardgods.com

Translation of Sun Tsu's "The Art of War" by Lionel Giles, published 1910.

Table of Contents

INTRODUCTION & WELCOME 1
01 CALCULATIONS 2
02 WAGING WAR 7
03 PLANNING ATTACKS 11
04 TACTICAL DISPOSITIONS 16
05 ENERGY 20
06 WEAKNESS AND STRENGTH 24
07 MANEUVERING 31
08 VARIATION IN TACTICS 37
09 MANEUVERS 40
10 TERRAIN 47
11 THE NINE SITUATIONS 53
12 ATTACK BY FIRE 64
13 USE OF SPIES 68
NOTES 72

Concept of pool 72

Defining the Intelligent player 72

Energy cycle 74

Other books by the author …

- Why Pool Hustlers Win
- Table Map Library
- Safety Toolbox
- Cue Ball Control Cheat Sheets
- Advanced Cue Ball Control Self-Testing Program
- Drills & Exercises for Pool & Pocket Billiards
- The Art of War versus The Art of Pool
- 3 Cushion Billiards Championship Shots (a series)
- Carom Billiards: Some Riddles & Puzzles
- Carom Billiards: MORE Riddles & Puzzles
- The Psychology of Losing – Tricks, Traps & Sharks
- The Art of Team Coaching
- The Art of Personal Competition
- The Art of Politics & Campaigning
- The Art of Marketing & Promotion
- Kitchen God's Guide for Single Guys

Introduction & welcome

The words of the famous and ancient Chinese general Sun Tzu have been read, studied, and applied by millions of students of warfare and those who compare their livelihood to be a similar life and death competition. Many advisors to the movers and shakers of the world have made their fortunes by converting Sun Tzu's words into the strategies and tactics of business and politics.

Many aspects of this 2500 year old treatise on how to wage war have a direct application to the tactics and strategies used in games played upon pocket billiard tables. This book is a presentation of those similarities. For the differences between actual war and pool, read the *Concept of pool* in the **Notes** section at the end of the book.

Sun Tzu's comments that do not have a similar match in the competitions of pool are still included. In order to study this properly, read the words of Sun Tzu's Art of War in the *ITALIC* font. Then, to learn its particular application in pool, read the corresponding commentary of the Art of Pool in the REGULAR font.

Read the first part, then the second. Stop and consider how the information can be used in your playing strategies and tactics. With the new viewpoint, reconsider the choices you made in your past competitions.

As you become aware of these new ways of thinking, your viewpoint will shift and adjust. You will see aspects of the game that previously were hidden. These discoveries belong to you and you alone. This is your personal voyage of discovery that leads to your new realization. The application of that knowledge will stay with you until the last day you ever pick up a stick.

01 Calculations

> **Commentary:** Much of the philosophy put forth in this book depends on learning to make wise decisions. It is not skills that are important - any skill can be learned through simple repetition; it is the use of your wise decisions. The study to learn mastery can only begin when you decide to become the Intelligent player. That can only occur when you realize that well-designed strategies and capable tactics are the greatest part of the Green Game.

The art of war is of vital importance to the State. It is a matter of life and death, a road either to safety or to ruin. Hence it is a subject of inquiry which can on no account be neglected.

> The art of pool is of vital importance to you. Your enthusiasm and passion is a major part of your life. When you win it brings joy to the day. When you lose, it is a negative experience causing a depressing viewpoint of life.
>
> Regardless of joy or depression, the participants come back to the table. The game and challenge is a great matter.

The art of war, then, is governed by five constant factors, to be taken into account in one's deliberations, when seeking to determine the conditions obtaining in the field. These are:

- *Moral Law - causes the people to be in complete accord with their ruler, so that they will follow him regardless of their lives, undismayed by any danger.*

- *Heaven - signifies night and day, cold and heat, times and seasons.*

- *Earth - comprises distances, great and small; danger and security; open ground and narrow passes; the chances of life and death.*

- *Commander - stands for the virtues of wisdom, sincerity, benevolence, courage and strictness.*

- *Method and discipline - the marshaling of the army in its proper subdivisions, the graduations of rank among the officers, the maintenance of roads by which supplies may reach the army, and the control of military expenditure.*

These five heads should be familiar to every general: he who knows them will be victorious; he who knows them not will fail.

The learning of the art of pool depends on these six fundamental factors. These are the basics upon which you are able to become the Intelligent player.

- Experience. This begins from the time you first picked up a stick through today. It is the sum total of your successes and failures in the hundreds and thousands of shots made on the pool table.

- Physical skills. The physical skills are the level of control you have in cue ball spin and speed. The closer the results to your intentions, the greater the mastery of physical skills.

- Mental skills. These are the calculations used to develop strategic plans and apply the appropriate tactics. Such effort depends on a realistic analysis of self and opponent.

- Knowledge. Information gained from many sources. It is the analytical observations of your opponents and monitored matches. This is coordinated with information learned from tutors, mentors, instructors, books, videos, etc.

- Self-discipline. This maintains control of your emotions. It keeps you focused on the immediate tasks as you advance your intentions. It helps you keep impulsive behavior under control. It is summed up in a collection of rules – when followed, improves your chances of winning; and if not, regularly leads to less successful results.

- Wisdom. This is more important than skills – it is maturity, based on considering situations in their true light. It combines all of the above. It is advanced when you study your mistakes, work out the real reason why, and find solutions to prevent future repetitions.

The player who understands these will win the majority of the time.

Therefore, in your deliberations, when seeking to determine the military conditions, let them be made the basis of a comparison, in this wise:

- *Which of the two sovereigns is imbued with the Moral Law?*

- *Which of the two generals has most ability?*

- *With whom lie the advantages derived from Heaven and Earth?*

- *On which side is discipline most rigorously enforced?*
- *Which army is stronger?*
- *On which side are officers and men more highly trained?*
- *In which army is there the greater constancy both in reward and punishment?*

By means of these seven considerations I can forecast victory or defeat.

The general that hearkens to my counsel and acts upon it, will conquer: - let such a one be retained in command! The general that hearkens not to my counsel nor acts upon it, will suffer defeat: - let such a one be dismissed!

Another way to determine your chances of winning against any opponent is to consider:

- Which has the greater success in results?
- Which has the greater wisdom in choices?
- Which has the greater self discipline?
- Which has the greater variety of skills?
- Which has the greater years of playing?
- Which has more experience in competition?
- Which has the larger comfort zone versus chaos zone?

The Intelligent player will use this analysis to fine tune and adjust the game to compete more effectively. The Foolish player will not even be aware that such analysis exists or even considers it useful.

While heeding the profit of my counsel, avail yourself also of any helpful circumstances over and beyond the ordinary rules.

According as circumstances are favorable, one should modify one's plans.

As you follow the various advices and guidelines provided in this book, keep your eyes open for circumstances that provide opportunities for quick advancement even to the win. If an advantage is thrown into your path by the table layout or accidents by your opponent, stop to consider how best to make the best use of this unexpected gift.

All warfare is based on deception.

- *Hence, when able to attack, we must seem unable;*
- *When using our forces, we must seem inactive;*
- *When we are near, we must make the enemy believe we are far away;*
- *When far away, we must make him believe we are near.*
- *Hold out baits to entice the enemy. Feign disorder, and crush him.*
- *If he is secure at all points, be prepared for him. If he is in superior strength, evade him.*
- *If your opponent is of choleric temper, seek to irritate him. Pretend to be weak, that he may grow arrogant.*
- *If he is taking his ease, give him no rest. If his forces are united, separate them.*
- *Attack him where he is unprepared, appear where you are not expected.*

These military devices, leading to victory, must not be divulged beforehand.

On the battlefield of the table, certain rules should be used to guide your routine decisions and choices. Therefore:

- When you are the more skillful, show only enough to win.
- Hide your knowledge of your opponent's strengths and weaknesses.
- Do not reveal your strategic or tactical options
- Where possible, make perfect shot results appear to be accidental.
- When ready, appear not to be ready.
- Disguise or put down your own capabilities.

- If he is on a down side of the energy cycle, press the advantage quickly.

- If he has substantial skills, deny opportunities.

- If he is easily upset, create problems.

- If he is humble, admire and compliment.

- If he is relaxed, provide difficulties.

These rules enhance your chances for victory. Make sure your opponent does not suspect your efforts are tailored to his skills and style of play.

Now the general who wins a battle makes many calculations in his temple ere the battle is fought. The general who loses a battle makes but few calculations beforehand. Thus do many calculations lead to victory and few calculations to defeat: how much more no calculation at all! It is by attention to this point that I can foresee who is likely to win or lose.

Before entering an important competition, identify potential opponents and determine their strengths and weaknesses. Allow the maximum possible time to gather information through observation. The more details you collect, the better your situational decisions will be.

If you are lazy and otherwise do not spend the time to observe and note the skills and abilities of opponents you are sure to lose many games.

If you do not otherwise have a way to evaluate your opponent, then you must do so during the match. Immediately configure appropriate tests and observe the results. Such tests can include temptation shots, defensive efforts designed to determine his reactions. Far better to gather intelligence ahead of time.

02 Waging war

In the operations of war, where there are in the field a thousand swift chariots, as many heavy chariots, and a hundred thousand mail-clad soldiers, with provisions enough to carry them a thousand Li (500 km), the expenditure at home and at the front, including entertainment of guests, small items such as glue and paint, and sums spent on chariots and amour, will reach the total of a thousand ounces of silver per day. Such is the cost of raising an army of 100,000 men.

The requirements of a serious player are these:

- Two quality cue sticks (with spare shafts) in a case - one for playing, one for breaking.
- Playing accessories (chalk, tip dresser, gloves, towel, etc.)
- Adequate transportation
- Access to a practice table (10 hours a week recommended)
- Local tournament entries (2 per month, minimum)
- Competitive matches (2-3 per week)
- Snacks (enough to keep away any hunger pangs)
- Funds to pay for expenses
- Mentor (at least 30-40 years experience)
- Season-appropriate clothing

When you engage in actual fighting, if victory is long in coming, then men's weapons will grow dull and their ardor will be damped.

A long match or tournament can wear you down and reduce your ability to concentrate and maintain self-discipline.

If you lay siege to a town, you will exhaust your strength.

Again, if the campaign is protracted, the resources of the State will not be equal to the strain.

> Where possible, do not play long matches that take hours to complete. This extended effort will use up energy reserves. When exhausted, your ability to make effective choices diminishes.
>
> In a multiple day tournament, ensure you allow enough time for proper rest and well-balanced, leisurely meals. Other than necessary time to keep your skills tuned, use every opportunity to relax while you observe and learn about other players.

Now, when your weapons are dulled, your ardor damped, your strength exhausted and your treasure spent, other chieftains will spring up to take advantage of your extremity. Then no man, however wise, will be able to avert the consequences that must ensue.

> When you have burned through all of your energy and used up your resources, your next competitors will be there to take advantage of your inability to think and play at your best levels.

Thus, though we have heard of stupid haste in war, cleverness has never been seen associated with long delays.

There is no instance of a country having benefited from prolonged warfare.

> Players who hurry up their routines usually make many mistakes and do not get the results they intend.
>
> But, over-thinking table conditions and taking long times to make shooting decisions will not help win more games.

It is only one who is thoroughly acquainted with the evils of war that can thoroughly understand the profitable way of carrying it on.

> The lessons learned from the consequences of careless or short-term planning will teach you the importance of proper planning and well-executed shooting.

The skillful soldier does not raise a second levy, neither are his supply-wagons loaded more than twice.

> As you play through your competitions, pace your playing routine. Conserve energy in order to have sufficient focus throughout the session.

Bring war material with you from home, but forage on the enemy. Thus the army will have food enough for its needs.

> On the road or otherwise attending away competitions, bring all you need with you, including extra equipment. Use local resources to provide consumables (food and rest).

Poverty of the State exchequer causes an army to be maintained by contributions from a distance. Contributing to maintain an army at a distance causes the people to be impoverished.

On the other hand, the proximity of an army causes prices to go up; and high prices cause the people's substance to be drained away.

When their substance is drained away, the peasantry will be afflicted by heavy exactions.

With this loss of substance and exhaustion of strength, the homes of the people will be stripped bare, and three-tenths of their income will be dissipated; while Government expenses for broken chariots, worn-out horses, breast-plates and helmets, bows and arrows, spears and shields, protective mantles, draught-oxen and heavy wagons, will amount to four-tenths of its total revenue.

Hence a wise general makes a point of foraging on the enemy. One cartload of the enemy's provisions is equivalent to twenty of one's own, and likewise a single picul of his provender is equivalent to twenty from one's own store.

> When playing on remote locations, any immediate winnings can be used to offset costs. Far better to have opponents provide the funds necessary for sustenance and rest.

Now in order to kill the enemy, our men must be roused to anger; that there may be advantage from defeating the enemy, they must have their rewards.

> When playing an opponent, it is necessary that you recognize this: "There are no friends on the table." To win, you must set aside fear and trepidation. Bring your best effort forward. Your reward will be that you played your best.

Therefore in chariot fighting, when ten or more chariots have been taken, those should be rewarded who took the first. Our own flags should be substituted for those of the enemy, and the chariots mingled and used in conjunction with ours. The captured soldiers should be kindly treated and kept.

> Extend your appreciation to the pool hall employees and owners/managers, referees, tournament directors, and other organizers. Your recognition is minor payment, but will be appreciated far beyond the effort. They may also provide assistance in unknown or unexpected ways.

This is called, using the conquered foe to augment one's own strength.

In war, then, let your great object be victory, not lengthy campaigns.

> Keep control of expenses so that winnings are not dissipated unwisely. In such circumstances, treat opponents who provide these funds with respect and courtesy.

Thus it may be known that the leader of armies is the arbiter of the people's fate, the man on whom it depends whether the nation shall be in peace or in peril.

> It is important to understand the consequences of your behavior and to guard excessive reactions to wins and losses. In this way you do not create antagonisms or other ill-feelings. Be known as a person of even temperament.

03 Planning attacks

In the practical art of war, the best thing of all is to take the enemy's country whole and intact; to shatter and destroy it is not so good. So, too, it is better to capture an army entire than to destroy it, to capture a regiment, a detachment or a company entire than to destroy them.

> Always allow your opponent to retain his dignity in defeat. Do not, during or after the competition, humiliate him either by attitude or words.
>
> Engendering bad feelings gives reason for him and his allies to find ways to defeat you, directly or indirectly. If you create ill-wishers, eventually they will be of sufficient numbers and influence to cause actual harm, either financially or to your reputation. Far better that, when triumphant, you are generous and benevolent towards your opponent. (If your opponent is an ass, maintain outward courtesy, but it is acceptable to take great personal satisfaction in winning.)

Hence to fight and conquer in all your battles is not supreme excellence; supreme excellence consists in breaking the enemy's resistance without fighting.

> Winning against opponents is not the greatest pleasure. The true enjoyment is winning because of your management and control of the table through the application of superior strategy and tactics.

Thus the highest form of generalship is to baulk the enemy's plans; the next best is to prevent the junction of the enemy's forces; the next in order is to attack the enemy's army in the field; and the worst policy of all is to besiege walled cities.

> The best competitive approach uses strategies of offense and defense tailored to your opponent, combined with fluid tactical responses to table conditions. The next best is a straight-forward continuous denial of opportunities. The worst approach is the use of total offense without regard to consequences.

The rule is, not to besiege walled cities if it can possibly be avoided. The preparation of mantlets, movable shelters, and various implements of war, will take up three whole months; and the piling up of mounds over against the walls will take three months more.

The general, unable to control his irritation, will launch his men to the assault like swarming ants, with the result that one-third of his men are slain, while the town still remains untaken. Such are the disastrous effects of a siege.

> The standard operational rule is to not provide easy wins to your opponent through poor control or lazy thinking. Always intentionally analyze, plan, select, and manage your game play and execution.
>
> Do not become reckless or distressed when you have no opportunities to advance. Continue your careful attention to preventing your opponent from advancing. Impatience will result in disaster.
>
> If you abandon self-discipline, you will fall prey to emotions, such as anger, frustration, irritation, even resignation. This will cause you to make bad choices and poor decisions. As a result you will miss and throw away game winning opportunities. A secondary consequence is that you make the entire effort of competition a waste of time and energy. Shooting without discipline leads to disaster.

Therefore the skillful leader subdues the enemy's troops without any fighting; he captures their cities without laying siege to them; he overthrows their kingdom without lengthy operations in the field.

With his forces intact he will dispute the mastery of the Empire, and thus, without losing a man, his triumph will be complete. This is the method of attacking by stratagem.

> Use strategies adapted to your opponent's abilities and craft clever tactics to control the table. When you force your opponent to react to your actions, he will make errors in skill and judgment to your benefit.

It is the rule in war, if our forces are ten to the enemy's one, to surround him; if five to one, to attack him; if twice as numerous, to divide our army into two.

If equally matched, we can offer battle; if slightly inferior in numbers, we can avoid the enemy; if quite unequal in every way, we can flee from him.

Hence, though an obstinate fight may be made by a small force, in the end it must be captured by the larger force

> These are the principles of selecting strategies.

- If you are the superior, win the competition without delay.

- If you are the better, be vigilant in your playing. Otherwise any miss can be a gift to your opponent.

- If equal in skill, determine your opponent's comfort/chaos zones, advance in small steps, and utilize defensive tactics to deny opportunities.

- If your skill is the lesser, be more pessimistic about your comfort/chaos zones, and plan all shots as two-way.

- If he is the overwhelming superior player, focus only on defense. Switch to offense only when you are SURE you can make the shot AND advance to the next. Force him to work harder than he expects. Study his responses and make notes of shots to practice. Afterwards, thank him for the lessons and that you look forward to another match in the future.

Therefore, it is important that you control yourself in your game choices and personal behaviors at all times. When you do not, you will lose.

Now the general is the bulwark of the State; if the bulwark is complete at all points, the State will be strong; if the bulwark is defective, the State will be weak.

As the Intelligent player, you are personally responsible for all well executed shots that lead to wins. You are also responsible for all the errors and mistakes that lead to losses. It is these that require the greater of your attention. Study every misstep in detail. Identify the individual reasons (usually more than one) for the failure. It is this focused post-shot analysis that ensures you shall become stronger and more dangerous.

There are three ways in which a ruler can bring misfortune upon his army:

- *By commanding the army to advance or to retreat, being ignorant of the fact that it cannot obey. This is called hobbling the army.*

- *By attempting to govern an army in the same way as he administers a kingdom, being ignorant of the conditions which obtain in an army. This causes restlessness in the soldier's minds.*

• By employing the officers of his army without discrimination, through ignorance of the military principle of adaptation to circumstances. This shakes the confidence of the soldiers.

But when the army is restless and distrustful, trouble is sure to come from the other feudal princes. This is simply bringing anarchy into the army, and flinging victory away.

There are many ways to destroy your ability to compete. These are the three most common:

- Abandon your self-discipline.
- Consume alcohol or drugs during competition.
- Play without sufficient rest.

When your mind is unable to coordinate your body, your opponents will take advantage. When you cannot control your impulses, you throw away any chance of winning.

Thus we may know that there are five essentials for victory:

- *He will win who knows when to fight and when not to fight.*
- *He will win who knows how to handle both superior and inferior forces.*
- *He will win whose army is animated by the same spirit throughout all its ranks.*
- *He will win who, prepared himself, waits to take the enemy unprepared.*
- *He will win who has military capacity and is not interfered with by the sovereign.*

Victory lies in the knowledge of these five points.

There are five factors that help predict who will win the majority of games.

- The player who knows when to play offensively, and when to play defensively.
- The player who knows how to use cushions, angles, and spins to manage table positions.

- The player who knows how to precisely manage control of the cue ball.
- The player who is patient when there are no opportunities.
- The player who is self-disciplined and is not distracted by others.

Success is a consequence of possessing these abilities.

Hence the saying:

- *If you know the enemy and know yourself, you need not fear the result of a hundred battles.*
- *If you know yourself but not the enemy, for every victory gained you will also suffer a defeat.*
- *If you know neither the enemy nor yourself, you will succumb in every battle.*

Therefore, the reality is:

- One who knows what the opponent can and cannot do and knows his own strengths and limitations will win the majority of all matches.
- One who does not know the opponent but knows his own strengths and weaknesses will win about half the time.
- One who does not know the opponent and does not know his limitations will lose most of the matches.

04 Tactical dispositions

The good fighters of old first put themselves beyond the possibility of defeat, and then waited for an opportunity of defeating the enemy.

To secure ourselves against defeat lies in our own hands, but the opportunity of defeating the enemy is provided by the enemy himself.

> To advance your skills requires discipline, study and training. This is how to become a tough and skilled competitor. What is not under your control is when or how your opponent makes mistakes. You can provide opportunities for him to make mistakes, but it is the opponent who must commit the error in skill or judgment. The majority of your wins occur because your opponent made one or more mistakes. (Rarely do you win solely on your offensive capabilities.)

Thus the good fighter is able to secure himself against defeat, but cannot make certain of defeating the enemy.

> Preparations can be made for many contingencies. Plans can be developed to handle any imaginable situation. But no level of preparation can cause an opponent to make an error. You must be alert for this prospect when it becomes available.

Hence the saying: One may know how to conquer without being able to do it.

> A player can be known for making skillful shots, but cannot often win.

Security against defeat implies defensive tactics; ability to defeat the enemy means taking the offensive. Standing on the defensive indicates insufficient strength; attacking, a superabundance of strength.

> Preventing your opponent from having easy opportunities is accomplished with defensive tactics. This is necessary until the table layout is within your abilities to complete to a win, when you are then able to take the offensive.

The general who is skilled in defense hides in the most secret recesses of the earth; he who is skilled in attack flashes forth from the topmost heights of heaven. Thus on the one hand we have ability to protect ourselves; on the other, a victory that is complete.

> When you are skilled in defensive tactics, you can easily deny your opponent any easy success. When an opening is finally available, you can pounce on the chance and drive to the win.

To see victory only when it is within the ken of the common herd is not the acme of excellence. Neither is it the acme of excellence if you fight and conquer and the whole Empire says, "Well done!" To lift an autumn hair is no sign of great strength; to see the sun and moon is no sign of sharp sight; to hear the noise of thunder is no sign of a quick ear.

What the ancients called a clever fighter is one who not only wins, but excels in winning with ease. Hence his victories bring him neither reputation for wisdom nor credit for courage. He wins his battles by making no mistakes. Making no mistakes is what establishes the certainty of victory, for it means conquering an enemy that is already defeated.

> To complete an easy table layout with balls close to pockets and a simple run-out pattern is not a sign of astute playing ability or a sign of skill. To pocket the winning game ball that an opponent left in the jaws is not a sign of a wise player.

> The Intelligent player wins matches with effective choices. He can win without having to demonstrate great skills. He can win because he makes fewer mistakes than his opponent. He can win by playing defensive shots when required. He can win by limiting his opponent's opportunities.

Hence the skillful fighter puts himself into a position which makes defeat impossible, and does not miss the moment for defeating the enemy.

> The Intelligent player possesses a prepared set of responses for many common table situations. This readiness allows opportunities to be immediately exploited when the opportunity is available.

Thus it is that in war the victorious strategist only seeks battle after the victory has been won, whereas he who is destined to defeat first fights and afterwards looks for victory.

> The Intelligent player wins consistently because of self-discipline and patience. When beginning any type of competition, the conditions of victory are already in place. The Foolish player enters a match without plans and many of his efforts are ineffective.

The consummate leader cultivates the Moral Law, and strictly adheres to method and discipline; thus it is in his power to control success.

The Intelligent player strives to improve skills, and gain both experience and knowledge. Practice time is dedicated to improving discovered deficiencies. To develop analysis skills, time is devoted to observing matches, identifying and selecting responses and comparing those selections to the results. Both physical and mental skills are continuously practiced.

In respect of military method, we have, firstly, Measurement; secondly, Estimation of quantity; thirdly, Calculation; fourthly, Balancing of chances; fifthly, Victory. Measurement owes its existence to Earth; Estimation of quantity to Measurement; Calculation to Estimation of quantity; Balancing of chances to Calculation; and Victory to Balancing of chances.

The factors in successful competitions are:

- Accurate self-knowledge of skills, limitations, and capabilities.
- Accurate observation and analysis of opponent's abilities.
- Designed strategies to fit your opponent.
- Clever tactics to advance your table development and restrict your opponent's options.
- Accurate analysis of the table layout.
- Effective pattern development.
- Correct determination and application of cue ball speed and spin.
- Proper body positioning.
- Precise and correct stroke execution.
- Consistent and rhythmic game play.

A victorious army opposed to a routed one, is as a pound's weight placed in the scale against a single grain. The onrush of a conquering force is like the bursting of pent-up waters into a chasm a thousand fathoms deep. So much for tactical dispositions.

Properly considered plans, executed with skill and discipline, provide an impetus towards victory. Each game win adds to your momentum. As strategic plans and tactical ploys succeed, you will gain confidence in your judgment, and likewise discourage your opponent.

05 Energy

The control of a large force is the same in principle as the control of a few men: it is merely a question of dividing up their numbers. Fighting with a large army under your command is nowise different from fighting with a small one: it is merely a question of instituting signs and signals.

> There is little real difference between the concept of pocketing three balls in a row and being able to run a table. This can be done with a plan, for example, dividing the table into groups of two and three ball sequences. With this plan, then the only requirement is to play each shot one at a time.
>
> **Note:** Your mistakes are your guide to what you need to learn.

To ensure that your whole host may withstand the brunt of the enemy's attack and remain unshaken - this is affected by maneuvers direct and indirect. That the impact of your army may be like a grindstone dashed against an egg - this is effected by the science of weak points and strong.

> The Intelligent player chooses offensive plans when table layouts are open. Where there are complications, defensive options are evaluated. In such cases, design your shots to manage your opponent's choices. This allows you to play your strengths against his weaknesses.

In all fighting, the direct method may be used for joining battle, but indirect methods will be needed in order to secure victory.

> Games are won with pocketing and cue ball positioning skills. It is rare to run out to a win from the opening of the game. This means that you must make flexible decisions as table conditions require.

Indirect tactics, efficiently applied, are inexhaustible as Heaven and Earth, unending as the flow of rivers and streams; like the sun and moon, they end but to begin anew; like the four seasons, they pass away to return once more. There are not more than five musical notes, yet the combinations of these five give rise to more melodies than can ever be heard. There are not more than five primary colors, yet in combination they produce more hues than can ever been seen. There are not more than five cardinal tastes, yet combinations of them yield more flavors than can ever be tasted.

> The same skills necessary to pocket balls and position the cue ball are easily adaptable to a wide variety of defensive shots that deny opportunities to your opponent. The choices available are limited only to your imagination and cleverness.

In battle, there are not more than two methods of attack - the direct and the indirect; yet these two in combination give rise to an endless series of maneuvers.

> In competition, the purpose of every shot choice is offensive, defensive, or the versatile two-way shot (offensive if successful, defensive if missed). The various choices for each shot offer an endless selection of options.

The direct and the indirect lead on to each other in turn. It is like moving in a circle — you never come to an end. Who can exhaust the possibilities of their combination?

> There is an endless variety of options that can be considered when playing any table layout. As you apply more consideration to strategic thinking and tactical responses, you will have greater and more complex possibilities to be considered.

The onset of troops is like the rush of a torrent which will even roll stones along in its course. The quality of decision is like the well-timed swoop of a falcon which enables it to strike and destroy its victim. Therefore the good fighter will be terrible in his onset, and prompt in his decision. Energy may be likened to the bending of a crossbow; decision, to the releasing of a trigger.

> The only energy applied in table billiards is that of the cue tip contacting the cue ball. The speed can range from a gentle half roll up through the massive force of a break shot. The actual applied speed depends on two factors - the decision in the mind, and the execution of trained muscles. When these are not coordinated, the results are unpredictable. Only when the body can execute precisely what the mind wants will you get the results intended. The Intelligent player strives to closely match the intention to the reality.

Amid the turmoil and tumult of battle, there may be seeming disorder and yet no real disorder at all; amid confusion and chaos, your array may be without head or tail, yet it will be proof against defeat.

> The layout of a table may appear to be chaotic. With proper thinking, the balls can be redefined into simple groups, each which

require analysis and a plan, even if it is to leave something unchanged. There will never be a situation that one or more plans cannot be developed that will benefit you and confuse opponents.

Simulated disorder postulates perfect discipline; simulated fear postulates courage; simulated weakness postulates strength. Hiding order beneath the cloak of disorder is simply a question of subdivision; concealing courage under a show of timidity presupposes a fund of latent energy; masking strength with weakness is to be effected by tactical dispositions.

To appear to be less skilled requires perfect discipline and focused intention. To appear incapable necessitates that shot decisions and their implementation must be pre-determined and executed carefully. This is necessary in order to implement certain tactical plans. Besides configuring this concept for your opponent, you must also be aware he might also do the same to you.

Thus one who is skillful at keeping the enemy on the move maintains deceitful appearances, according to which the enemy will act. He sacrifices something, that the enemy may snatch at it. By holding out baits, he keeps him on the march; then with a body of picked men he lies in wait for him.

The Intelligent player must be knowledgeable and skilled in distracting his opponent with table positioning problems and poor shot choices. Sometimes, he can allow his opponent an apparently easy run, knowing that it cannot be concluded, resulting in an open table to more easily win the game. Presenting these opportunities is as important as pocketing and positioning skills.

The clever combatant looks to the effect of combined energy, and does not require too much from individuals. Hence his ability to pick out the right men and to utilize combined energy. When he utilizes combined energy, his fighting men become as it were like unto rolling logs or stones. For it is the nature of a log or stone to remain motionless on level ground, and to move when on a slope; if four-cornered, to come to a standstill, but if round-shaped, to go rolling down. Thus the energy developed by good fighting men is as the momentum of a round stone rolled down a mountain thousands of feet in height. So much on the subject of energy.

The Intelligent player carefully rations his energy. He must maintain the same focus and intention throughout the match. He is careful to move slowly and not rush any action, no matter how simple. When given an opportunity to relax or take refreshment or sustenance, he takes full advantage. Then, when it is most needed to sustain the final effort, he has the strength and the reserves to complete the match successfully.

06 Weakness and strength

Whoever is first in the field and awaits the coming of the enemy, will be fresh for the fight; whoever is second in the field and has to hasten to battle will arrive exhausted.

> When coming to a competition, arrive early enough to scope out the playing environment (even if it is already familiar). Get a look at the competition listing to identify players you know and don't. Identify others who have also come early. Walk through the competition area, checking the tables, cushions, and pockets. When possible, run through some favorite drills, leisurely pocket several racks, just enough to start warming up. About an hour before the match starts, stop and find a comfortable location to relax. Observe late arrivals and judge their readiness.

Therefore the clever combatant imposes his will on the enemy, but does not allow the enemy's will to be imposed on him.

> The Intelligent player controls the opportunities that an opponent has. When you must let him come to the table, you select the layout you want to provide. Even as you do this, be watchful if he attempts to control your options.

By holding out advantages to him, he can cause the enemy to approach of his own accord; or, by inflicting damage, he can make it impossible for the enemy to draw near.

> During the opening of the match, force your opponent to demonstrate the extent of his skills. Provide tempting opportunities and observe the results. From these observations, you will know his comfort zones.

If the enemy is taking his ease, he can harass him; if well supplied with food, he can starve him out; if quietly encamped, he can force him to move. Appear at points which the enemy must hasten to defend; march swiftly to places where you are not expected.

> Provide these types of shots to your opponent when you allow him to come to the table. In this way, you can ensure he has few comfortable shots.
>
> - off the rail

- over another ball

- long distance

- sharp cuts

- difficult banks

These and others are designed to deny opportunities. Each one adds a small amount of psychological stress. A continuous series of these, over time, will weaken the intention to win.

An army may march great distances without distress, if it marches through country where the enemy is not.

When preparing for competition, do not add unnecessary pressure to yourself. Make all necessary preparations ahead of time. This will leave your mind at ease.

You can be sure of succeeding in your attacks if you only attack places which are undefended.

You can be sure of winning, when you only allow your opponent to shoot from positions that he has not mastered.

You can ensure the safety of your defense if you only hold positions that cannot be attacked.

When you have no opportunity to advance, leave such shots that your opponent will find very difficult or impossible to play. Focus on regaining the initiative.

Hence that general is skillful in attack whose opponent does not know what to defend; and he is skillful in defense whose opponent does not know what to attack.

When the opponent does not respond well to denial of opportunities, provide them in abundance. This adds chaos to his game and simplifies the process of winning.

O divine art of subtlety and secrecy! Through you we learn to be invisible, through you inaudible; and hence we can hold the enemy's fate in our hands.

The Intelligent player is both fluid and flexible in action. Plans must consider table layouts, truthful self assessment, and careful opponent analysis. The opponent can never know whether you will advance or defend or do both simultaneously.

You may advance and be absolutely irresistible, if you make for the enemy's weak points; you may retire and be safe from pursuit if your movements are more rapid than those of the enemy.

There are two ways an opponent can be confused and become reactive in his thinking. One way is overwhelming force (i.e., quickly winning several games in a row). The other is to continuously deny favorable circumstances.

If we wish to fight, the enemy can be forced to an engagement even though he be sheltered behind a high rampart and a deep ditch. All we need do is to attack some other place that he will be obliged to relieve. If we do not wish to fight, we can prevent the enemy from engaging us even though the lines of our encampment be merely traced out on the ground. All we need do is to throw something odd and unaccountable in his way.

An opponent can be "trained" to become reactive to your strategies and tactics. With few and poor openings for advancement, your opponents can not maintain rigid self-discipline. The result is an almost active effort to help you win.

By discovering the enemy's dispositions and remaining invisible ourselves, we can keep our forces concentrated, while the enemy's must be divided.

Determine your opponent's emotions while hiding your own. They are indicators of the level of self-discipline. The more emotions that are displayed, the easier will be the win.

When his emotions are under control, you must challenge him with difficult shots that require greater mental effort. The more of these that can be provided throughout the match, the greater your chances are of winning the match.

We can form a single united body, while the enemy must split up into fractions. Hence there will be a whole pitted against separate parts of a whole, which means that we shall be many to the enemy's few.

By carefully managing your energy and maintaining self-discipline, you will have the reserves necessary at the end of the match. Force your opponent to work harder early. He will be more easily distracted later in the match.

And if we are able thus to attack an inferior force with a superior one, our opponents will be in dire straits. The spot where we intend to fight must not be made known; for then the enemy will have to prepare against a possible attack at several different points; and his forces being thus distributed in many directions, the numbers we shall have to face at any given point will be proportionately few.

> When you observe that your opponent is distracted and unable to concentrate, you have an opening in which to win multiple games. He will have difficulty preventing you. Also observe his *energy cycles*. When you see the beginning of a down side, increase the pressure of your offensive efforts and apply effective defensive shots.

For should the enemy strengthen his van, he will weaken his rear; should he strengthen his rear, he will weaken his van; should he strengthen his left, he will weaken his right; should he strengthen his right, he will weaken his left. If he sends reinforcements everywhere, he will everywhere be weak.

> When players are good at offensive shots and cue ball positioning, they can be weak at defensive calculations. If they are good at close in cut shots, they can be weak with long table shots. Few players practice to learn all of the necessary skills to become a dangerous player. This leaves gaps in their skills or limitations in strategic analysis. The complexities of the Green Game ensure that few players are able to master all of the permutations. There is always some weakness to be identified.

Numerical weakness comes from having to prepare against possible attacks; numerical strength, from compelling our adversary to make these preparations against us.

> If your opponent is unable to initiate an offensive effort, you have limited his options.

Knowing the place and the time of the coming battle, we may concentrate from the greatest distances in order to fight.

> When you know where and when your competition will take place you can visit the place and become familiar with the playing environment. When you know who will be the competitors, you can research their skills and abilities.

But if neither time nor place be known, then the left wing will be impotent to succor the right, the right equally impotent to succor the left, the van unable to relieve the rear, or the rear to support the van.

> When the opponent is unknown, and you compete at an unfamiliar place, no specific preparations can be made. Because of these unknown factors, you may have to play a number of games cautiously in order to observe and gather sufficient information to make effective playing choices.

How much more so if the furthest portions of the army are anything under a hundred Li (50 km) apart, and even the nearest are separated by several Li! Though according to my estimate the soldiers of Yüeh exceed our own in number, that shall advantage them nothing in the matter of victory. I say then that victory can be achieved.

Though the enemy be stronger in numbers, we may prevent him from fighting. Scheme so as to discover his plans and the likelihood of their success.

> An opponent's skills may be many, but many might be hidden. When the opponent's skills and abilities are known, these can be countered. Configure appropriate tests to determine the range of skills.

Rouse him, and learn the principle of his activity or inactivity. Force him to reveal himself, so as to find out his vulnerable spots.

> Provoke your opponent with temptation shots to observe his responses. Present a range of difficult shots to understand his comfort/chaos zones.

Carefully compare the opposing army with your own, so that you may know where strength is superabundant and where it is deficient.

> Study your opponent's skills, both offensive and defensive. Compare them to your own and determine relative weaknesses and strengths.

In making tactical dispositions, the highest pitch you can attain is to conceal them; conceal your dispositions, and you will be safe from the prying of the subtlest spies, from the machinations of the wisest brains.

> Do not reveal the totality of your skills and knowledge. Conceal the outer edges of your comfort zones. To continue the deception, miss

some shots in situations where the apparent failure will not change the balance of the game against you.

How victory may be produced for them out of the enemy's own tactics - that is what the multitude cannot comprehend. All men can see the tactics whereby I conquer, but what none can see is the strategy out of which victory is evolved.

When you win by manipulating your opponent's weaknesses, few people understand how or why this happened. They observe the tactics you apply, but do not understand the strategies behind them. They also do not see or understand the conclusions that resulted from your observations.

Do not repeat the tactics which have gained you one victory, but let your methods be regulated by the infinite variety of circumstances.

The tactics used to defeat one opponent will not be the same as those used to defeat another. This is because every match has unique conditions and circumstances and every opponent has a different variety of skills. In this way, no opponent can know how you will play against him.

Military tactics are like unto water; for water in its natural course runs away from high places and hastens downwards. So in war, the way is to avoid what is strong and to strike at what is weak. Water shapes its course according to the nature of the ground over which it flows; the soldier works out his victory in relation to the foe whom he is facing. Therefore, just as water retains no constant shape, so in warfare there are no constant conditions.

Choices and decisions are always made based on the opponent and the table layout. Because you can be infinitely flexible, you cannot be predictable.

He who can modify his tactics in relation to his opponent and thereby succeed in winning, may be called a heaven-born captain.

Adjust your tactics to counter his strengths and display his weaknesses. Force him into situations where he is uncomfortable.

The five elements are not always equally predominant; the four seasons make way for each other in turn. There are short days and long; the moon has its periods of waning and waxing.

You are subject to the ups and downs of your *energy cycles*. When you are on the up side, your efforts will predominantly be offensive, when on the down side, mostly defensive. Also observe your opponent's cycles. Take appropriate actions as the two cycles cross-cross each other.

07 Maneuvering

Having collected an army and concentrated his forces, he must blend and harmonize the different elements thereof before pitching his camp

> At the competition, you must have sufficient self-discipline to keep your attention and focus on the game being played.

After that, comes tactical maneuvering, than which there is nothing more difficult.

> You must own a large library of tactical options. Many of the options will have been learned from difficult experiences.

The difficulty of tactical maneuvering consists in turning the devious into the direct, and misfortune into gain.

> Each of your shot choices must support both small and large goals, while also working to maintain necessary subterfuges.

Thus, to take a long and circuitous route, after enticing the enemy out of the way, and though starting after him, to contrive to reach the goal before him, shows knowledge of the artifice of deviation.

> The early part of the match must construct an image in your opponent's mind that you are less than you really are. This may include allowing one or more intentional losses. Subsequent to this, you can then focus on the management of the table to your benefit.

Maneuvering with an army is advantageous; with an undisciplined multitude, most dangerous.

> In the course of a match, maintain your self-discipline. Even a momentary distraction can lose one or more games. Do not provide your opponent with any unnecessary advantage.

If you set a fully equipped army in march in order to snatch an advantage, the chances are that you will be too late. On the other hand, to detach a flying column for the purpose involves the sacrifice of its baggage and stores.

> There will be situations when an unanticipated opportunity occurs. In such circumstances, previous plans will have to be abandoned while you take immediate advantage.

Thus, if you order your men to roll up their buff-coats, and make forced marches without halting day or night, covering double the usual distance at a stretch, doing a hundred li (50 km) in order to wrest an advantage, the leaders of all your three divisions will fall into the hands of the enemy. The stronger men will be in front, the jaded ones will fall behind, and on this plan only one-tenth of your army will reach its destination.

> If you lose your self-discipline and attempt a tactical plan that is well outside your abilities, you will sacrifice any advancement already made. The temptation is usually a perceived short cut to a win. This is a self-imposed trap of impatience. The result will rarely achieve your expectations and you have provided an easy opportunity for your opponent to win.

If you march fifty Li (25 km) in order to outmaneuver the enemy, you will lose the leader of your first division, and only half your force will reach the goal. If you march thirty Li (15 km) with the same object, two-thirds of your army will arrive.

> The lesser the time you spend on your selecting a shot, the fewer opportunities you will be able to recognize. If a normal evaluation routine averages 15 seconds to recognize and consider six options, if you allow 10 seconds you will identify three. If you allow five seconds, you will identify one.

We may take it then that an army

- *without its baggage-train is lost;*
- *without provisions it is lost;*
- *without bases of supply it is lost.*

> In this rationale,
> - if table analysis is eliminated, you will lose
> - If opponent analysis is eliminated, you will lose
> - if self-assessment is ignored, you will lose.
> - if proper pre-shot routine is not followed, you will lose
> - if shot consequences are not considered, you will lose

We cannot enter into alliances until we are acquainted with the designs of our neighbors.

> It is difficult to formulate table plans without understanding how an opponent handles problems and difficult layouts. It is also necessary to know how well he controls the cue ball.

We are not fit to lead an army on the march unless we are familiar with the face of the country - its mountains and forests, its pitfalls and precipices, its marshes and swamps. We shall be unable to turn natural advantage to account unless we make use of local guides.

> When faced with a difficult table layout only make decisions based on skills you have mastered. If you invent unproven tactics, you will make many mistakes.

In war, practice dissimulation, and you will succeed. Move only if there is a real advantage to be gained.

- *Whether to concentrate or to divide your troops, must be decided by circumstances.*
- *Let your rapidity be that of the wind, your compactness that of the forest.*
- *In raiding and plundering be like fire, in immovability like a mountain.*
- *Let your plans be dark and impenetrable as night, and when you move, fall like a thunderbolt.*

> The Intelligent player does not reveal his full capability. Only near the end of a match does an opponent get even a glimpse of your best skills. And you still want to disguise it as luck. In this way, you can:
>
> - adjust to any table layout
> - set sophisticated traps
> - control the cue ball with perfect speed and spin
> - move balls to intended locations
> - plan and execute patterns
> - win with ease

When you plunder a countryside, let the spoil be divided amongst your men; when you capture new territory, cut it up into allotments for the benefit of the soldiery.

> When you have placed in the money at tournaments, make sure you thank the supporting personnel, such as the tournament director, referees, etc. In some locations, an appropriate tip is acceptable.

Ponder and deliberate before you make a move. He will conquer who has learnt the artifice of deviation. Such is the art of maneuvering.

> When analyzing a table layout, take into consideration all factors to determine whether an offensive, defensive, or a two-way shot will be most effective. Manage the selection and execution with all due seriousness.

The Book of Army Management says: On the field of battle, the spoken word does not carry far enough: hence the institution of gongs and drums. Nor can ordinary objects be seen clearly enough: hence the institution of banners and flags.

Gongs and drums, banners and flags, are means whereby the ears and eyes of the host may be focused on one particular point.

The host thus forming a single united body, it is impossible either for the brave to advance alone, or for the cowardly to retreat alone. This is the art of handling large masses of men.

In night-fighting, then, make much use of signal-fires and drums, and in fighting by day, of flags and banners, as a means of influencing the ears and eyes of your army.

> \<no real comparison in the world of table billiards\>

A whole army may be robbed of its spirit; a commander-in-chief may be robbed of his presence of mind. Now a soldier's spirit is keenest in the morning; by noonday it has begun to flag; and in the evening, his mind is bent only on returning to camp.

A clever general, therefore, avoids an army when its spirit is keen, but attacks it when it is sluggish and inclined to return. This is the art of studying moods.

The abilities of all players operate on an *energy cycle*. When your opponent is on the up side, configure restrictions and limitations on his opportunities. When you are on the up side, aggressively push for the win. If your opponent is on the down side, advance towards the win. When you are on the down side, decrease the size of your comfort zones and slow down your rhythm.

Disciplined and calm, to await the appearance of disorder and hubbub amongst the enemy: - this is the art of retaining self-possession.

When your opponent is disciplined and calm, you must concentrate on preventing opportunities for him to win. When he loses focus and is shooting erratically, you can concentrate on offense.

To be near the goal while the enemy is still far from it, to wait at ease while the enemy is toiling and struggling, to be well-fed while the enemy is famished: — this is the art of husbanding one's strength.

When you are near the end of the match and on the hill while your opponent is several games out, retain your self-discipline. Do not begin celebrating. Pacing your efforts will get you to the end with reserves to finish well.

To refrain from intercepting an enemy whose banners are in perfect order, to refrain from attacking an army drawn up in calm and confident array: - this is the art of studying circumstances.

However you opponent is playing (well or poorly), do not let him change or otherwise dictate your playing style. Many players, when an opponent is doing well, discard their proven style and adopt the other. If you play according to his behavior, you are at the disadvantage. Continue your regular table analysis and shot selection process. Remain fluid in your response to table layouts.

It is a military axiom:

- *Not to advance uphill against the enemy.*

- *Nor to oppose him when he comes downhill.*

- *Do not pursue an enemy who simulates flight; do not attack soldiers whose temper is keen.*

- *Do not swallow bait offered by the enemy. Do not interfere with an army that is returning home.*

- *When you surround an army, leave an outlet free. Do not press a desperate foe too hard.*

Such is the art of warfare.

The principles of competition are:

- When an opponent is on the up side of his energy cycle, apply constant denial tactics.
- On the up side of your energy cycle, be aggressive. On your down side, be defensive.
- Do not allow an opponent to dictate choices or otherwise change your plans.
- When the table is configured to your opponent's best interest, rearrange the layout.
- Do not underestimate an opponent's skills.
- Do not overestimate your skills.
- Consider each shot to be of life or death importance.
- Be patient in your deliberation.
- Be careful in your execution.

This is the art of pool.

08 Variation in tactics

In war, the general receives his commands from the sovereign, collects his army and concentrates his forces

> When you prepare for a match you must align your priorities. Exclude thoughts of life outside the pool table, relationships, work, and everything else. For the length of the competition, your world is the pool table.

When in difficult country, do not encamp. In country where high roads intersect, join hands with your allies. Do not linger in dangerously isolated positions. In hemmed-in situations, you must resort to stratagem. In a desperate position, you must fight.

> On arriving at a competition, maintain a low profile. Greet friends and acquaintances in a low-key manner. Use distant courtesy as a shield to eliminate attention. This ensures you do not reveal unnecessary information and opponents do not consider you to be dangerous – until at the table.

There are roads which must not be followed, armies which must not be attacked, towns which must not be besieged, positions which must not be contested, commands of the sovereign which must not be obeyed.

> There are table layouts where you should not attempt an offensive pattern. There are shots that you should not attempt to pocket. There are ball patterns that should be managed.

The general who thoroughly understands the advantages that accompany variation of tactics knows how to handle his troops.

> The Intelligent player knows his capabilities and limitations and knows how to evaluate any type of table layout. He knows when to choose offensive tactics and when defense is the proper choice.

The general who does not understand these, may be well acquainted with the configuration of the country, yet he will not be able to turn his knowledge to practical account.

> There are table layouts where you may know what must be done, but are unable to implement the necessary solution.

So, the student of war who is unversed in the art of varying his plans, even though he be acquainted with the Five Advantages, will fail to make the best use of his men.

> If you do not know your strengths or limitations, even if you are an excellent shot maker, you will not be able to effectively compete.

Hence in the wise leader's plans, considerations of advantage and of disadvantage will be blended together.

- *If our expectation of advantage be tempered in this way, we may succeed in accomplishing the essential part of our schemes.*

- *If, on the other hand, in the midst of difficulties we are always ready to seize an advantage, we may extricate ourselves from misfortune.*

> Therefore, the Intelligent player considers tactics to fit the table layout, his abilities, the opponent's skills, and the playing circumstances.
>
> - When in comfort zones - play offensively and advance the game towards the win.
>
> - When in chaos zones, play defensively and where possible prepare the table for the next inning.

Reduce the hostile chiefs by inflicting damage on them; make trouble for them, and keep them constantly engaged; hold out specious allurements, and make them rush to any given point.

> Analyze your opponent to determine his comfort/chaos zones. Identify obvious weaknesses in his patterns and plans. In the process of discovery, offer tempting opportunities that expose his limitations and invite failure.

The art of war teaches us to rely:

- *Not on the likelihood of the enemy's not coming, but on our own readiness to receive him;*

- *Not on the chance of his not attacking, but rather on the fact that we have made our position unassailable.*

> So the art of pool means that you:

- Do not depend on your opponent being unprepared, but depend on your readiness to compete against him.

- Do not depend on your opponent being defensive or weak, but depend on your abilities to deny opportunities.

There are five dangerous faults which may affect a general:

- *recklessness, which leads to destruction;*

- *cowardice, which leads to capture;*

- *a hasty temper, which can be provoked by insults;*

- *a delicacy of honor which is sensitive to shame;*

- *over-solicitude for his men, which exposes him to worry and trouble.*

These are the five besetting sins of a general, ruinous to the conduct of war. When an army is overthrown and its leader slain, the cause will surely be found among these five dangerous faults. Let them be a subject of meditation.

There are five dangerous faults to avoid:

- Selecting a shot without proper analysis.

- Shooting too quickly or too hard.

- Playing defense too often.

- Responding negatively to your own mistakes or perceived bad luck.

- Allowing outside factors to distract your attention.

These are deadly faults in any player, and are disastrous in competition at any level. Generally, almost all match and competition loses can be attributed to one or more of these dangerous faults. Consider ways in which these can be avoided.

09 Maneuvers

We come now to the question of encamping the army, and observing signs of the enemy.

- *Pass quickly over mountains, and keep in the neighborhood of valleys. Camp in high places, facing the sun. Do not climb heights in order to fight. So much for mountain warfare.*

- *After crossing a river, you should get far away from it. When an invading force crosses a river in its onward march, do not advance to meet it in mid-stream. It will be best to let half the army get across, and then deliver your attack. If you are anxious to fight, you should not go to meet the invader near a river which he has to cross. Moor your craft higher up than the enemy, and facing the sun. Do not move up-stream to meet the enemy. So much for river warfare.*

- *In crossing salt-marshes, your sole concern should be to get over them quickly, without any delay. If forced to fight in a salt-marsh, you should have water and grass near you, and get your back to a clump of trees. So much for operations in salt-marshes.*

- *In dry, level country, take up an easily accessible position with rising ground to your right and on your rear, so that the danger may be in front, and safety lie behind. So much for campaigning in flat country.*

These are the four useful branches of military knowledge which enabled the Yellow Emperor to vanquish four several sovereigns.

> On analyzing your opponent to determine how best to manage him, these are the elements to be identified:
>
> - Determine the quality of his shot execution: stroke, stance, rhythm, speed, accuracy, cue ball control.
>
> - Determine his BPI (balls per inning) average.
>
> - Confirm the quality of his abilities to make good tactical choices.
>
> - Confirm his abilities to manage the cue ball from position to position.
>
> - Identify bad habits that can be used: jacking the stick up on a rail shot, awkward stance, super long bridge, poor follow-through, etc.

- Evaluate his personality and attitude. Is he quick tempered? Is he easily upset on missing? Is he a fast or slow player?

- Look for his comfort/chaos zone. What angles and distances are difficult? Any weaknesses on banking or kicking?

These are aspects of your opponent that you must study and learn. With this information, you can manage any table layout to avoid his strengths and play to his weaknesses.

All armies prefer high ground to low and sunny places to dark. If you are careful of your men, and camp on hard ground, the army will be free from disease of every kind, and this will spell victory. When you come to a hill or a bank, occupy the sunny side, with the slope on your right rear. Thus you will at once act for the benefit of your soldiers and utilize the natural advantages of the ground.

The Intelligent player can enjoy playing opponents who have obvious weaknesses, such as poor positioning abilities, poor planning, and a limited imagination.

But do not assume all players have these limitations. To prepare for those competitors, use practice times effectively and for best results. Do not waste the time in casual competition. Rather, 10 minutes of focused practice time is more helpful to your skills than two hours of casual play.

When, in consequence of heavy rains up-country, a river which you wish to ford is swollen and flecked with foam, you must wait until it subsides.

When your opponent is shooting at his best levels, be patient. Work not to win, but to deny chances for him to advance. His energy cycle will eventually change and you can recover control of the table.

Country in which there are precipitous cliffs with torrents running between, deep natural hollows, confined places, tangled thickets, quagmires and crevasses, should be left with all possible speed and not approached.

When you have bad table layouts with clusters and blocked pockets, improve the table by carefully improving your table, while leaving problems for your opponent. Make improvements using carefully planned and precise shots. Consider consequences of each play.

While we keep away from such places, we should get the enemy to approach them; while we face them, we should let the enemy have them on his rear.

> While you make tactical decisions to clear up problem areas, always leave one ball trapped and allow your opponent to open it up for you.

If in the neighborhood of your camp there should be any hilly country, ponds surrounded by aquatic grass, hollow basins filled with reeds, or woods with thick undergrowth, they must be carefully routed out and searched; for these are places where men in ambush or insidious spies are likely to be lurking. When the enemy is close at hand and remains quiet, he is relying on the natural strength of his position.

> If your opponent plays numerous defense shots, observe his precision. How effective is the result? Are the shots choices simple or over-complicated? Look for weakness in skill or planning. Where the opportunity arises, engage in safety battles to distract his attention while you prepare the layout for a win.

When he keeps aloof and tries to provoke a battle, he is anxious for the other side to advance. If his place of encampment is easy of access, he is tendering a bait.

> Watch carefully to determine if he is capable of developing strategies. (Most players can only consider tactical responses.) If so, watch for traps and temptations and select ways to counter them. Much of your choices will depend on your estimate of his table intelligence.

Movement amongst the trees of a forest shows that the enemy is advancing. The appearance of a number of screens in the midst of thick grass means that the enemy wants to make us suspicious. The rising of birds in their flight is the sign of an ambuscade. Startled beasts indicate that a sudden attack is coming. When there is dust rising in a high column, it is the sign of chariots advancing; when the dust is low, but spread over a wide area, it betokens the approach of infantry. When it branches out in different directions, it shows that parties have been sent to collect firewood. A few clouds of dust moving to and fro signify that the army is encamping.

> Watch your opponent carefully to study his mental process. Look for reactions to your efforts and other changes in behavior. See how he responds to various types of problems.

A careless opponent does not maintain his self-discipline. He will be distracted and look at other tables, converse with individuals, or otherwise not focus on the table. He will not have good self-discipline either. Ignore attempts to engage you in conversation. When you must say something, do so without looking at him. (While he is not paying attention to your shooting, advance quickly. He won't recognize that you just played above his expectations.)

Humble words and increased preparations are signs that the enemy is about to advance.

If he is quiet and playing close attention to the table activity, he is looking for advantageous opportunities.

Violent language and driving forward as if to the attack are signs that he will retreat.

If he demonstrates anger or frustration, he has already lost the game.

When the light chariots come out first and take up a position on the wings, it is a sign that the enemy is forming for battle.

If he increases the time that he takes for table analysis, he will play at a higher level of intensity.

Peace proposals unaccompanied by a sworn covenant indicate a plot.

If he talks with you about any subject other than the necessary communications in the course of the game, he is attempting to shark you.

When there is much running about and the soldiers fall into rank, it means that the critical moment has come.

If he changes his pre-shot routine, he has corrected some fundamental that will allow greater accuracy.

When some are seen advancing and some retreating, it is a lure.

When he shortened the time spent on his table analysis and is focused, he is implementing a plan.

When the soldiers stand leaning on their spears, they are faint from want of food. If those who are sent to draw water begin by drinking themselves, the army is suffering from thirst.

If your opponent starts eyeing the bar or food counter he is hungry or thirsty.

If the enemy sees an advantage to be gained and makes no effort to secure it, the soldiers are exhausted.

If he misses simple shots or selects shots that have no advantage, he is mentally/physically tired.

If birds gather on any spot, it is unoccupied. Clamor by night betokens nervousness.

If he is treating the game with a casual manner, his mind is away from the game. If he moans and groans over every bad result, he is frustrated and afraid to lose.

If there is disturbance in the camp, the general's authority is weak. If the banners and flags are shifted about, sedition is afoot. If the officers are angry, it means that the men are weary.

If he is not focused, his self-discipline is weak. If fidgeting in his chair or commenting negatively about the game he is afraid of losing.

When an army feeds its horses with grain and kills its cattle for food, and when the men do not hang their cooking-pots over the camp-fires, showing that they will not return to their tents, you may know that they are determined to fight to the death.

When you notice that his eyes are direct and focused and he ignores outside distractions, he is serious about winning. When every movement around the table is sure and smooth without thought, he is in the zone and will play shots and patterns efficiently.

The sight of men whispering together in small knots or speaking in subdued tones points to disaffection amongst the rank and file.

If he wraps himself in silence with a frown or petulant look on his face, he has lost his desire to win.

Too frequent rewards signify that the enemy is at the end of his resources.

<no real comparison in the world of table billiards>

Too many punishments betray a condition of dire distress.

> If he is cranky at everyone and is generally disagreeable, he fears the loss of the match.

To begin by bluster, but afterwards to take fright at the enemy's numbers, shows a supreme lack of intelligence.

> If the guy is a jerk when things are good, he'll be an ass when he loses.

When envoys are sent with compliments in their mouths, it is a sign that the enemy wishes for a truce.

> If he offers to buy a drink, he needs a break and is trying to distract you from your focus.

If the enemy's troops march up angrily and remain facing yours for a long time without either joining battle or taking themselves off again, the situation is one that demands great vigilance and circumspection.

> If your opponent acts in an unusual manner, but does not play worse, watch carefully both his demeanor and actions. He is planning a subterfuge.

If our troops are no more in number than the enemy, that is amply sufficient; it only means that no direct attack can be made.

> If the skills between you and your opponent are approximately equal, there will be no quick resolution. The match will continue to be close to the final game.

What we can do is simply to concentrate all our available strength, keep a close watch on the enemy, and obtain reinforcements.

> Maintain confidence in your skills. Keep faith in your abilities. Stick with your chosen strategy and apply proper tactics. Do not relax or otherwise assume victory.

He who exercises no forethought but makes light of his opponents is sure to be captured by them.

> An opponent without a plan will lose.

If soldiers are punished before they have grown attached to you, they will not prove submissive; and, unless submissive, they will be practically useless. If, when the soldiers have become attached to you, punishments are not enforced, they will still be useless. Therefore soldiers must be treated in the first instance with humanity, but kept under control by means of iron discipline. This is a certain road to victory.

> If you do not practice properly, there will be few shots that can be trusted to be effective. Only with sufficient practice to develop shots that you know can be properly executed will you be able to play effectively.

If in training soldiers commands are habitually enforced, the army will be well-disciplined; if not, its discipline will be bad. If a general shows confidence in his men but always insists on his orders being obeyed, the gain will be mutual.

> During any practice, apply a specific plan to improve one or several specific abilities. Over weeks, months, and years, you will develop skills that are precise.

10 Terrain

We may distinguish six kinds of terrain, to wit: (1) Accessible ground; (2) entangling ground; (3) temporizing ground; (4) narrow passes; (5) precipitous heights; (6) positions at a great distance from the enemy.

- *(1) Ground which can be freely traversed by both sides is called accessible. With regard to ground of this nature, be before the enemy in occupying the raised and sunny spots, and carefully guard your line of supplies. Then you will be able to fight with advantage.*

- *(2) Ground which can be abandoned but is hard to re-occupy is called entangling. From a position of this sort, if the enemy is unprepared, you may sally forth and defeat him. But if the enemy is prepared for your coming, and you fail to defeat him, then, return being impossible, disaster will ensue.*

- *(3) When the position is such that neither side will gain by making the first move, it is called temporizing ground. In a position of this sort, even though the enemy should offer us an attractive bait, it will be advisable not to stir forth, but rather to retreat, thus enticing the enemy in his turn; then, when part of his army has come out, we may deliver our attack with advantage.*

- *(4) With regard to narrow passes, if you can occupy them first, let them be strongly garrisoned and await the advent of the enemy. Should the enemy forestall you in occupying a pass, do not go after him if the pass is fully garrisoned, but only if it is weakly garrisoned.*

- *(5) With regard to precipitous heights, if you are beforehand with your adversary, you should occupy the raised and sunny spots, and there wait for him to come up. If the enemy has occupied them before you, do not follow him, but retreat and try to entice him away.*

- *(6) If you are situated at a great distance from the enemy, and the strength of the two armies is equal, it is not easy to provoke a battle, and fighting will be to your disadvantage.*

These six are the principles connected with Earth. The general who has attained a responsible post must be careful to study them.

> Depending on your skills, table options can be wide open, open, clustered, difficult, and do or die. These are some ways in which you can address these situations to make wiser choices.

- A wide open table has only a few balls in easy to make positions. The pattern for the run-out is simple. Do not become careless. Ensure that every action is planned and executed under control.

- An open table is one that can be run (dependent on the balls per inning average. The process to run-out should be started but will need back-up options if any shot gets out of line.

- A clustered table means one or more balls are tied up in a group that prevents a run-out. When to open the cluster depends on table circumstances and opponent's skills.

- A difficult table has multiple problems, such as balls in clusters, blocking pockets, and in dead zones. This type of layout requires a plan to develop properly that considers both offensive and defensive choices at each shot choice.

- A do or die table occurs when you must run out to the end. If you don't, you lose.

It is your responsibility to recognize the conditions and apply the correct tactics.

Now an army is exposed to six several calamities, not arising from natural causes, but from faults for which the general is responsible. These are: (1) flight, (2) insubordination, (3) collapse, (4) ruin, (5) disorganization, (6) rout.

- *(1) Other conditions being equal, if one force is hurled against another ten times its size, the result will be the flight of the former.*

- *(2) When the common soldiers are too strong and their officers too weak, the result is insubordination.*

- *(3) When the officers are too strong and the common soldiers too weak, the result is collapse.*

- *(4) When the higher officers are angry and insubordinate, and on meeting the enemy, give battle on their own account from a feeling of resentment, before the commander-in-chief can tell whether or not he is in a position to fight, the result is ruin.*

- *(5) When the general is weak and without authority; when his orders are not clear and distinct; when there are no fixed duties assigned to officers and men, and the ranks are formed in a slovenly haphazard manner, the result is utter disorganization.*

- *(6) When a general, unable to estimate the enemy's strength, allows an inferior force to engage a larger one, or hurls a weak detachment against a powerful one, and neglects to place picked soldiers in the front rank, the result must be a rout.*

These are six ways of courting defeat, which must be carefully noted by the general who has attained a responsible post.

In competition, there are several ways in which you can be defeated. These are your responsibilities to identify them as early as possible in order to attempt to counter them.

- If the opponent has superior skills (see note).
- If you are on the down side of your energy cycle.
- If you are tired or hungry.
- If you are unstable because of some outside influence (angry, upset, saddened, etc.).
- If you are careless of the consequences.
- If the game is of no importance to you.
- If you do not properly analyze the opponent.
- If you do not consider multiple tactics for each shot.
- If you are distracted from some activity (sharked).
- If you are in any other mental state than required for proper focus and attention.

Any of these conditions plus others that not enumerated here will lead to a defeat. Some defeats are more important than others. And some defeats should never have occurred. Other times, your attempts to recover begin too late in the match to be effective.

Note: when the opponent is of superior skill, it is important that you fight to the bitter end with all your strength and tenacity. At the same time, watch closely to see how your opponent responds to each attempt to slow him down.

> Look for elements that can be added to your knowledge for future use. Make notes of shots and setups to practice and master. In all, if defeated, accept it as the price to pay for learning new responses and actions.

The natural formation of the country is the soldier's best ally; but a power of estimating the adversary, of controlling the forces of victory, and of shrewdly calculating difficulties, dangers and distances, constitutes the test of a great general.

> To test the opponent, set up a sequence of shots to determine his comfort/chaos zones. Examples of such testing shots are long distances, sharp cuts, and banks. With this information, you can configure table setups that deny opportunities to your opponent. You will also know when to play an offensive or defensive shot.

He who knows these things, and in fighting puts his knowledge into practice, will win his battles. He who knows them not, nor practices them, will surely be defeated.

If fighting is sure to result in victory, then you must fight, even though the ruler forbid it; if fighting will not result in victory, then you must not fight even at the ruler's bidding.

> In competition, when the win is inevitable, you may want to slow down and extend the innings. It may be needed to offer a more palatable loss to your opponent.

> When a defeat is inevitable, you may want to concede the match rather than struggle to little avail. Or, in such a situation, change the reason you are playing from winning (no longer possible) to learning.

> Use available innings for defensive shots, or re-arranging the layout. Then observe the results. These tactics may reveal weaknesses that can be used in a later competition to win.

The general who advances without coveting fame and retreats without fearing disgrace, whose only thought is to protect his country and do good service for his sovereign, is the jewel of the kingdom.

Regard your soldiers as your children, and they will follow you into the deepest valleys; look upon them as your own beloved sons, and they will stand by you even unto death. If, however, you are indulgent, but unable to make your authority felt; kind-hearted, but unable to enforce your commands; and incapable, moreover, of quelling disorder: then your soldiers must be likened to spoilt children; they are useless for any practical purpose.

> The Intelligent player always maintains the ambition to become as skilled as possible and to learn as much as possible. Every mistake, every loss, every setback has within it a lesson to be learned.
>
> When deficiencies are noted, work to remove them. Where plans fail, consider the whys. Without attention to these, your skills will not advance and your wisdom will not improve.

If we know that our own men are in a condition to attack, but are unaware that the enemy is not open to attack, we have gone only halfway towards victory.

> If you delay testing the opponent early in the match, when the knowledge is finally learned, it may be too late to use it to your best advantage.

If we know that the enemy is open to attack, but are unaware that our own men are not in a condition to attack, we have gone only halfway towards victory.

> If you understand your opponent's skills and weaknesses, but cannot consistently move the cue ball to the correct locations, you reduce your chances of winning.

If we know that the enemy is open to attack, and also know that our men are in a condition to attack, but are unaware that the nature of the ground makes fighting impracticable, we have still gone only halfway towards victory.

> If you understand the opponent and his abilities, but do not make good choices based on the table layout, you will allow him opportunities to win.

Hence the experienced soldier, once in motion, is never bewildered; once he has broken camp, he is never at a loss.

> With knowledge of your skills and knowledge of your opponent's skills, you have immense flexibility.

Hence the saying: If you know the enemy and know yourself, your victory will not stand in doubt; if you know Heaven and know Earth, you may make your victory complete.

> When you know yourself, and you know the opponent, you will win most of your competitive matches.

11 The nine situations

The art of war recognizes nine varieties of ground: (1) dispersive ground, (2) facile ground, (3) contentious ground, (4) open ground, (5) ground of intersecting highways, (6) serious ground, (7) difficult ground;, (8) hemmed-in ground, (9) desperate ground

- *(1) When a chieftain is fighting in his own territory, it is dispersive ground.*

- *(2) When he has penetrated into hostile territory, but to no great distance, it is facile ground.*

- *(3) Ground the possession of which imports great advantage to either side, is contentious ground.*

- *(4) Ground on which each side has liberty of movement is open ground.*

- *(5) Ground which forms the key to three contiguous states, so that he who occupies it first has most of the Empire at his command, is a ground of intersecting highways.*

- *(6) When an army has penetrated into the heart of a hostile country, leaving a number of fortified cities in its rear, it is serious ground.*

- *(7) Mountain forests, rugged steeps, marshes and fens - all country that is hard to traverse: this is difficult ground.*

- *(8) Ground which is reached through narrow gorges, and from which we can only retire by tortuous paths, so that a small number of the enemy would suffice to crush a large body of our men: this is hemmed in ground.*

- *(9) Ground on which we can only be saved from destruction by fighting without delay, is desperate ground.*

Therefore,

- *(1) On dispersive ground, fight not.*

- *(2) On facile ground, halt not.*

- *(3) On contentious ground, attack not.*

- *(4) On open ground, do not try to block the enemy's way.*
- *(5) On the ground of intersecting highways, join hands with your allies.*
- *(6) On serious ground, gather in plunder.*
- *(7) In difficult ground, keep steadily on the march.*
- *(8) On hemmed-in ground, resort to stratagem.*
- *(9) On desperate ground, fight.*

    There are many types of competitions that can be played.

    - Where two players compete in their home pool hall, this is a home competition. The competitive terms will vary from friendly matches to small bets.
    - Where one goes to an opponent's pool hall, usually with a team for a set of matches, this is a league competition.
    - Where one competes in a locally scheduled event, you will have some familiarity with the location. This is a small tournament competition.
    - Where tables are available as part of community services, such as a senior center, this is casual competition.
    - Where qualifier events are scheduled, usually for entry to higher levels, these are regional tournament competitions.
    - Where you enter an unfamiliar bar with unknown rules, this is friendly bar competition (only as long as no bets are being made).
    - Where you play at a bar at a much lower class level that you are familiar with, this is a dangerous bar competition.
    - Where you play at expensive high class pool halls, you are subject to higher standards of play and dress. This is an upper social class competition.
    - Where you compete in tournaments with a one loss and out, this is a single elimination tournament.

- Where you compete in a tournament where two losses are required to lose, this is a double elimination tournament.

- Where you compete against every entrant, this is a round robin tournament.

- Where you play a competition with a big entry fee, you are in a high skill level tournament.

- Where you are betting small amounts on sequential matches, you are in a small stakes competition.

- Where you are placing large amounts on your ability to win, you are in a high stakes competition.

Therefore,

- Respect the unofficial standards of conduct of the places you play

- If you don't know the rules of play, ask.

- Dress and act appropriately.

- Do not over-consume alcohol.

- Observe new environments carefully before participating.

- Make friends with local regulars to develop advisors and allies.

- Do not act foolish, brash, or pushy.

Those who were called skillful leaders of old knew how to drive a wedge between the enemy's front and rear; to prevent cooperation between his large and small divisions; to hinder the good troops from rescuing the bad, the officers from rallying their men.

When the enemy's men were scattered, they prevented them from concentrating; even when their forces were united, they managed to keep them in disorder.

> The Intelligent player knows how to control the table and thereby give his opponent only the table layouts he wants to provide. He knows when it is appropriate to be on the offensive and when to be on the defensive.

> He is able to limit his opponent's choices and otherwise constantly offering only poor table layouts.

When it was to their advantage, they made a forward move; when otherwise, they stopped still.

> When layouts are favorable, then advance towards the win. When not favorable, apply such maneuvers that can improve the layout or cause the opponent to do so.

If asked how to cope with a great host of the enemy in orderly array and on the point of marching to the attack, I should say: "Begin by seizing something which your opponent holds dear; then he will be amenable to your will."

> If your opponent shows great skills early in the competition, what should you do? The answer is to be patient, while you do what can be done to prevent his advancement. In other words, complicate the layout and deny chances to advance. Maintain your strategies. Eventually, his *energy cycle* will move downward and you will be ready to take advantage and advance yourself.

Rapidity is the essence of war: take advantage of the enemy's unreadiness, make your way by unexpected routes, and attack unguarded spots.

> The essential factor in effective competition is flexibility. Take advantage of opportunities. Prevent your opponent from advancing.

The following are the principles to be observed by an invading force: The further you penetrate into a country, the greater will be the solidarity of your troops, and thus the defenders will not prevail against you.

Make forays in fertile country in order to supply your army with food.

> <no real comparison in the world of table billiards>

Carefully study the well-being of your men, and do not overtax them. Concentrate your energy and hoard your strength. Keep your army continually on the move, and devise unfathomable plans.

> Reserve your energies throughout the match. Save your strength for the end of the match when the intensity will rise. Keep yourself alert and apply appropriate tactics as dictated by the table layout.

Throw your soldiers into positions whence there is no escape, and they will prefer death to flight. If they will face death, there is nothing they may not achieve. Officers and men alike will put forth their uttermost strength.

Soldiers when in desperate straits lose the sense of fear. If there is no place of refuge, they will stand firm. If they are in hostile country, they will show a stubborn front. If there is no help for it, they will fight hard.

> When your attention is entirely focused on the immediate game and match, your strategies and tactics you have no opportunities to experience fear.

Thus, without waiting to be marshaled, the soldiers will be constantly on the qui vive; without waiting to be asked, they will do your will; without restrictions, they will be faithful; without giving orders, they can be trusted.

> Depend on your developed skills and proven abilities. Those can be trusted and used with confidence.

Prohibit the taking of omens, and do away with superstitious doubts. Then, until death itself comes, no calamity need be feared.

> Do not depend on random actions around you to be defined as an omen for success or failure.

If our soldiers are not overburdened with money, it is not because they have a distaste for riches; if their lives are not unduly long, it is not because they are disinclined to longevity.

> <no real comparison in the world of table billiards>

On the day they are ordered out to battle, your soldiers may weep, those sitting up bedewing their garments, and those lying down letting the tears run down their cheeks. But let them once be brought to bay, and they will display the courage of a Chu or a Kuei.

> On the day and time of competition, you may feel trepidation and otherwise suffer nervous emotions. But when the competition actually begins, such feelings will dissipate when you become focused on the details of the game.

The skillful tactician may be likened to the shuai-jan. Now the shuai-jan is a snake that is found in the Ch'ang mountains. Strike at its head, and you will be attacked by its tail; strike at its tail, and you will be attacked by its head; strike at its middle, and you will be attacked by head and tail both.

No matter what your opponent tries to do to prevent your success, your tactical responses counter his actions. No matter how he tries to restrict your options, you end up restricting his choices.

Asked if an army can be made to imitate the shuai-jan, I should answer, Yes. For the men of Wu and the men of Yüeh are enemies; yet if they are crossing a river in the same boat and are caught by a storm, they will come to each other's assistance just as the left hand helps the right.

<no real comparison in the world of table billiards>

Hence it is not enough to put one's trust in the tethering of horses, and the burying of chariot wheels in the ground. The principle on which to manage an army is to set up one standard of courage which all must reach. How to make the best of both strong and weak - that is a question involving the proper use of ground.

Organize your responses to fit your opponent. When he is strong, deny opportunities to advance, where he is weak, take advantage. Where you can advance, do so. Where you cannot, play defensive tactics suitable to the layout.

Thus the skillful general conducts his army just as though he were leading a single man, willy-nilly, by the hand.

Manage your game with self-discipline. Ration your energies and stay alert. Make decisions without emotion focus, and attention. You can then devote yourself to the game without distraction.

He must be able to mystify his officers and men by false reports and appearances, and thus keep them in total ignorance.

At no time reveal to your opponent the thought processes used to determine your playing tactics.

By altering his arrangements and changing his plans, he keeps the enemy without definite knowledge. By shifting his camp and taking circuitous routes, he prevents the enemy from anticipating his purpose.

When unable to advance, continuously apply tactics and responses that leave difficulties for your opponent. Do not allow him to know you are using tailored tactics.

At the critical moment, the leader of an army acts like one who has climbed up a height and then kicks away the ladder behind him. He carries his men deep into hostile territory before he shows his hand.

He burns his boats and breaks his cooking-pots; like a shepherd driving a flock of sheep, he drives his men this way and that, and nothing knows whither he is going.

To muster his host and bring it into danger: — this may be termed the business of the general.

> At the mid-point of each game, you must begin continuous close monitoring for an opportunity to go all out on the offensive and run out to the win.

The different measures suited to the nine varieties of ground; the expediency of aggressive or defensive tactics; and the fundamental laws of human nature: these are things that must most certainly be studied.

> When the competition begins, commit yourself and trust your skills, knowledge, and experience. The strategies are determined by your opponent's abilities. The tactics are based on table layouts. Be patient and maintain self-discipline. These are your responsibilities.

When invading hostile territory, the general principle is,

- *Penetrating deeply brings cohesion;*

- *Penetrating but a short way means dispersion.*

- *When you leave your own country behind, and take your army across neighborhood territory, you find yourself on critical ground.*

- *When there are means of communication on all four sides, the ground is one of intersecting highways.*

- *When you penetrate deeply into a country, it is serious ground.*

- *When you penetrate but a little way, it is facile ground.*

- *When you have the enemy's strongholds on your rear, and narrow passes in front, it is hemmed-in ground.*

- *When there is no place of refuge at all, it is desperate ground.*

Therefore,

- *On dispersive ground, I would inspire my men with unity of purpose.*
- *On facile ground, I would see that there is close connection between all parts of my army.*
- *On contentious ground, I would hurry up my rear.*
- *On open ground, I would keep a vigilant eye on my defenses.*
- *On ground of intersecting highways, I would consolidate my alliances.*
- *On serious ground, I would try to ensure a continuous stream of supplies.*
- *On difficult ground, I would keep pushing on along the road.*
- *On hemmed-in ground, I would block any way of retreat.*
- *On desperate ground, I would proclaim to my soldiers the hopelessness of saving their lives.*

For it is the soldier's disposition to offer an obstinate resistance when surrounded, to fight hard when he cannot help himself, and to obey promptly when he has fallen into danger.

We cannot enter into alliance with neighboring princes until we are acquainted with their designs.

> <no real comparison in the world of table billiards>

We are not fit to lead an army on the march unless we are familiar with the face of the country — its mountains and forests, its pitfalls and precipices, its marshes and swamps. We shall be unable to turn natural advantages to account unless we make use of local guides.

> If you do not have the skills to maneuver the cue ball carefully and with effective control, you will have difficulties. You must have the skills and abilities to precisely control how and where the cue ball will stop.

To be ignorant of any one of the following four or five principles does not befit a warlike prince.

When a warlike prince attacks a powerful state, his generalship shows itself in preventing the concentration of the enemy's forces. He overawes his opponents, and their allies are prevented from joining against him.

> When playing an aggressive opponent, select such tactics that prevent him from applying on his best skills. Exhaust his focus by forcing him to constantly shoot in situations that are uncomfortable.

Hence he does not strive to ally himself with all and sundry, nor does he foster the power of other states. He carries out his own secret designs, keeping his antagonists in awe. Thus he is able to capture their cities and overthrow their kingdoms.

> Maintain an innocence when setting up difficulties for your opponent. Let him believe his problems are caused by unlucky circumstances.

Bestow rewards without regard to rule, issue orders without regard to previous arrangements; and you will be able to handle a whole army as though you had to do with but a single man.

Confront your soldiers with the deed itself; never let them know your design. When the outlook is bright, bring it before their eyes; but tell them nothing when the situation is gloomy.

> Present your opponents with results that require him to use of skills that have not been well practiced.

Place your army in deadly peril, and it will survive; plunge it into desperate straits, and it will come off in safety.

For it is precisely when a force has fallen into harm's way that is capable of striking a blow for victory.

> There are times when, in desperate situations during a match when you must drive for the win.

> You may have a difficult starting position, but you must put everything you have into driving to the win. Anything less and you fail.

Success in warfare is gained by carefully accommodating ourselves to the enemy's purpose.

> Adapt your strategies to your opponent's strengths and weaknesses.

By persistently hanging on the enemy's flank, we shall succeed in the long run in killing the commander-in-chief. This is called ability to accomplish a thing by sheer cunning.

> When you can limit your opponent's choices with difficult layouts and poor cue ball positions, you entice him to become careless. When he is careless, you can win.

On the day that you take up your command, block the frontier passes, destroy the official tallies, and stop the passage of all emissaries.

> When the competition begins, set aside all outside concerns and play your game.

Be stern in the council-chamber, so that you may control the situation.

> Do not second guess yourself when faced with occasional setbacks.

If the enemy leaves a door open, you must rush in.

> When your opponent leaves an opening, take advantage of it.

Forestall your opponent by seizing what he holds dear, and subtly contrive to time his arrival on the ground.

> Prevent openings for your opponent to advance. Of all things, prevent him from having easy wins. In this way, you prepare him to lose.

Attack what he values most.

> Determine what part of the process of playing is most important to him. Is he prideful? It can be about precision cue ball control, pocketing skills, positioning skills, etc. Disrupt his opportunities to accomplish this.

Walk in the path defined by rule, and accommodate yourself to the enemy until you can fight a decisive battle.

> Follow your plans and adjust your tactics to the table until you are able to win.

At first, then, exhibit the coyness of a maiden, until the enemy gives you an opening; afterwards emulate the rapidity of a running hare, and it will be too late for the enemy to oppose you.

In the beginning, play cautiously. When he leaves you an opening, do so quickly so that he has no opportunity to prevent the loss.

12 Attack by fire

Note: Pool competitions do not require the use of fire as a tactical tool. Therefore, the focus used by *The Art of* Pool segment for this chapter is based on responses to table layouts. Every shot requires an analysis and a decision. The varieties of options depend on the complexity of the layout and your experience in addressing similar circumstances. In this way, consider the use of tactical difficulties to create dismaying circumstances as the equivalent of using fire to destroy an opponent's abilities to fight.

There are five ways of attacking with fire.

- *First is to burn soldiers in their camp;*

- *Second is to burn stores;*

- *Third is to burn baggage-trains;*

- *Fourth is to burn arsenals and magazines;*

- *Fifth is to hurl dropping fire amongst the enemy.*

In order to carry out an attack with fire, we must have means available. The material for raising fire should always be kept in readiness.

There are tactical plans that can be applied to any table layout:

- Full offensive - a decision to win the game in one inning, purely by offense.

- Partial offensive - a pre-defined set of balls are pocketed and then a defensive tactic is applied.

- Two-way - speed and spin is calculated so that if made, the cue ball is positioned for another shot. If missed, the cue ball position is at a poor location.

- Full defense - the basic purpose is to provide a table layout that the opponent will find, at the least, uncomfortable.

There is a proper season for making attacks with fire, and special days for starting a conflagration. The proper season is when the weather is very dry; the special days are those when the moon is in the constellations of the Sieve, the Wall, the Wing or the Cross-bar; for these four are all days of rising wind.

There are appropriate times when to create tactical difficulties. Many choices are made because of your poor positioning skills. Other choices are created when unforeseen problems occurred. The need to initiate a denial of choice can simply have occurred intentionally or even accidently by the opponent.

Such decisions require a reality check on your abilities, and a consideration of the consequences if you come up short of your goal. Decisions to use defense require a reality check on your opponent's abilities and what he cannot handle.

In attacking with fire, one should be prepared to meet five possible developments:

- *When fire breaks out inside the enemy's camp, respond at once with an attack from without.*

- *If there is an outbreak of fire, but the enemy's soldiers remain quiet, bide your time and do not attack.*

- *When the force of the flames has reached its height, follow it up with an attack, if that is practicable; if not, stay where you are.*

- *If it is possible to make an assault with fire from without, do not wait for it to break out within, but deliver your attack at a favorable moment.*

- *When you start a fire, be to windward of it. Do not attack from the leeward.*

A wind that rises in the daytime lasts long, but a night breeze soon falls.

In every army, the five developments connected with fire must be known, the movements of the stars calculated, and a watch kept for the proper days.

The tactics you choose also depend on the variations of the energy cycle. These are also considerations about what shot to choose and how to execute it well.

- When your opponent is on a down cycle or distracted, become more aggressive.

- When he is on an up cycle, become more defensive.

- When you are on the up side, become more aggressive.

- When you are on the down side, become more defensive.

Hence those who use fire as an aid to the attack show intelligence; those who use water as an aid to the attack gain an accession of strength. By means of water, an enemy may be intercepted, but not robbed of all his belongings.

Select tactics based on the facts, not on emotions. (Decisions made while enthused assume you cannot fail, those made while depressed assume you will fail.) This includes your analysis of your opponent's abilities, your skills, his energy cycle, your energy cycle, and the table layout. Also, consider the consequences of each shooting choice if not successful. If successful, retain a memory of it. If unsuccessful, study the shot and determine what would have been a better choice. Remember that.

Unhappy is the fate of one who tries to win his battles and succeed in his attacks without cultivating the spirit of enterprise; for the result is waste of time and general stagnation.

If you make decisions while impatient, you will have wasted your time and efforts.

Hence the saying: The enlightened ruler lays his plans well ahead; the good general cultivates his resources.

- *Move not unless you see an advantage; use not your troops unless there is something to be gained; fight not unless the position is critical.*

- *No ruler should put troops into the field merely to gratify his own spleen; no general should fight a battle simply out of pique.*

- *If it is to your advantage, make a forward move; if not, stay where you are.*

Do not let emotions control you. Maintain your patience through self-discipline in these circumstances:

- If several innings pass with no advancement, an advantage will soon become available.

- A complicated table layout is handled ball by ball.

- Good luck that benefits your opponent now will change to bad luck later.

- Do not think a few successes will extend indefinitely into the future.

- Do not think that a few failures will extend indefinitely into the future.

No ruler should put troops into the field merely to gratify his own spleen; no general should fight a battle simply out of pique.

> Do not change playing styles because of any setback. Do not make decisions based on anger or irritation.

If it is to your advantage, make a forward move; if not, stay where you are.

> When an opportunity arises, advance your game. If not, be patient.

Anger may in time change to gladness; vexation may be succeeded by content.

> Problems of all types will eventually resolve themselves. What is a difficult layout during one inning will become a simple and easy layout later.

But a kingdom that has once been destroyed can never come again into being; nor can the dead ever be brought back to life. Hence the enlightened ruler is heedful, and the good general full of caution. This is the way to keep a country at peace and an army intact.

> Think, evaluate, and consider lessons learned from past successes and failures. Above all, do not be hasty. The majority of matches and competitions will be won by using your intelligence and not by fear or anger. To maintain your ability to compete requires above all, self discipline. This is how you maintain a winning record.

13 Use of spies

> **NOTE:** The following adaptation of this chapter is defined as you doing your own spying. It is your observations and correct conclusions that will lead to being the effective competitor. Information learned can be strategic or tactical. When you gain strategic information that changes your tactical choices when you play against your opponent. New tactical information modifies your choices and how you implement them.

Raising a host of a hundred thousand men and marching them great distances entails heavy loss on the people and a drain on the resources of the State. The daily expenditure will amount to a thousand ounces of silver.

> It is expensive to go on the road to compete.

There will be commotion at home and abroad, and men will drop down exhausted on the highways. As many as seven hundred thousand families will be impeded in their labor.

> The preparation process will disrupt your playing routines.

Hostile armies may face each other for years, striving for the victory which is decided in a single day. This being so, to remain in ignorance of the enemy's condition simply because one grudges the outlay of a hundred ounces of silver in honors and emoluments, is the height of inhumanity. One who acts thus is no leader of men, no present help to his sovereign, no master of victory.

> Spend some funds on introducing yourself to local players and observers. Take time to buy a couple of drinks and make friends from whom you can collect local information.

Thus, what enables the wise sovereign and the good general to strike and conquer, and achieve things beyond the reach of ordinary men, is foreknowledge.

> Having advanced knowledge about competitors can give you an edge. From such information, you can determine skill levels, problem areas, habits, and other useful details.

Now this foreknowledge cannot be elicited from spirits; it cannot be obtained inductively from experience, nor by any deductive calculation. Knowledge of the enemy's dispositions can only be obtained from other men.

Information must be researched. It cannot be assembled from rumor or hearsay. It should be collected as close to the source as possible.

Hence the use of spies, of whom there are five classes: (1) Local spies; (2) inward spies; (3) converted spies; (4) doomed spies; (5) surviving spies.

When these five kinds of spy are all at work, none can discover the secret system. This is called "divine manipulation of the threads". It is the sovereign's most precious faculty.

- *(1) Having local spies means employing the services of the inhabitants of a district.*

- *(2) Having inward spies, making use of officials of the enemy.*

- *(3) Having converted spies, getting hold of the enemy's spies and using them for our own purposes.*

- *(4) Having doomed spies, doing certain things openly for purposes of deception, and allowing our own spies to know of them and report them to the enemy.*

- *(5) Surviving spies, finally, are those who bring back news from the enemy's camp.*

Hence it is that with none in the whole army are more intimate relations to be maintained than with spies. None should be more liberally rewarded. In no other business should greater secrecy be preserved.

> There are multiple ways in which to gather information. Some resources are internet searches, blogs, social networks (i.e., Facebook, Twitter, etc.), videos on various video web sites, newsgroups, friends who might know other friends, local railbirds, etc. The broader your friendship reaches, the more resources you have for information about players, competitions, reputations, etc.

Spies cannot be usefully employed without a certain intuitive sagacity. They cannot be properly managed without benevolence and straightforwardness. Without subtle ingenuity of mind, one cannot make certain of the truth of their reports. Be subtle and subtle to use your spies for every kind of business.

> Every pool hall has individuals who will be happy to provide information. Confirm negative information from more than one source. Treat good sources as valuable friends.

If a secret piece of news is divulged by a spy before the time is ripe, he must be put to death together with the man to whom the secret was told.

> When an acquaintance reveals information that you want to be held back, cut off any future communications. They have proven themselves to be faithless and disloyal.

Whether the object be to crush an army, to storm a city, or to assassinate an individual, it is always necessary to begin by finding out the names of the attendants, the aides-de-camp, the door-keepers and sentries of the general in command. Our spies must be commissioned to ascertain these.

> When getting ready to compete in any location, learn about the top players and get to know people who have information about their playing abilities.

The enemy's spies who have come to spy on us must be sought out, tempted with bribes, led away and comfortably housed. Thus they will become converted spies and available for our service. It is through the information brought by the converted spy that we are able to acquire and employ local and inward spies. It is owing to his information, again, that we can cause the doomed spy to carry false tidings to the enemy. Lastly, it is by his information that the surviving spy can be used on appointed occasions. The end and aim of spying in all its five varieties is knowledge of the enemy; and this knowledge can only be derived, in the first instance, from the converted spy. Hence it is essential that the converted spy be treated with the utmost liberality.

> The best information sources when coming into new playing environments are the regulars and the employees of the business where the competition takes place. Treat them with special consideration so that they are willing to provide details.

Of old, the rise of the Yin dynasty was due to I Chih who had served under the Hsia. Likewise, the rise of the Chou dynasty was due to Lü Ya who had served under the Yin.

> <no real comparison in the world of table billiards>

Hence it is only the enlightened ruler and the wise general who will use the highest intelligence of the army for purposes of spying, and thereby they achieve great results. Spies are a most important element in war, because on them depends an army's ability to move.

With good information, you can make informed decisions that will improve your knowledge. Take time to develop the network of friends who can provide that information.

Notes

The text of *The Art of War* used for this edition was translated by Lionel Giles and published 1910.

Concept of pool

In the universe of table billiards, two players do not directly interact with each other. There are no simultaneous actions, responses, and overall development of resources to achieve victory that is the common implementation of war.

A player can only come to the table when the other player was unable to win. When one player has won the game, it is over and the opponent has no opportunity to challenge the win.

Even within these considerable constraints, there are still opportunities for a player to take control of the flow of the game, even when competing against someone with superior skills. This is accomplished by manipulating the placements of object balls and the cue ball. When the opponent does come to the table and has very few options, it will generally occur because of the player's intention.

The purpose is two-fold. One is to prevent the opponent from shooting out to a win. The other is to force an unplanned error that will provide an opportunity for you to achieve victory.

There are enough facets to the calculations and considerations of the Green Game that would satisfy the most Machiavellian goals of strategic development and tactical implementation. This is where the Art of Pool is at its greatest glory. In no other type of sport can one gain the greatest amount of experience in indirectly manipulating others through the seemingly simplistic games of table billiards.

Defining the Intelligent player

This is the player who is skilled in offensive and defensive abilities, who understands force and accuracy. His knowledge base is extensive and wide. Every mistake is an opportunity to learn and advance towards the unattainable goal of perfection - perfect position and perfect accuracy. Above all – he is self-disciplined and constantly evaluates data as data.

Hundreds and thousands of hours in competition and upon the practice table are required just to begin to gain wisdom. There will be many mistakes on the playing table, in assumptions, and the experiences of interacting with players at all levels.

Eventually, a person will gain enough wisdom to have taken the first steps towards the top of the mountain, only to realize he is still in the foothills. The will probably be the day that he realizes that his devotion to this game will continue for the rest of his life. There will not be any turning back at that point.

Energy cycle

The underlying natural operations of the human body are on a series of up and down cycles that looks very similar to the patterns of a sine wave (see example). This is a natural flow that affects your entire life waking and sleeping. In pool, you are subject to the same flow which can be directly observed in the effectiveness of your playing ability.

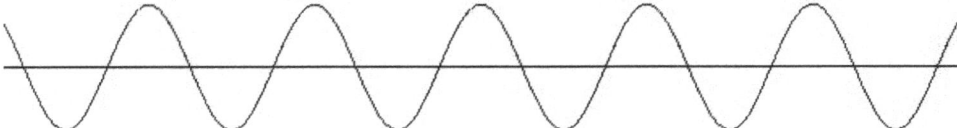

When you are on your up cycle, you are more accurate and precise in your shots, sometimes very noticeably. Even the balls seem to roll your way. Game wins occur with wonderful regularity and everyone is admiring you and your skills. It can get thrilling.

On the down side of the cycle, you have difficulties and problems. Shots are harder, routine patterns are tougher to follow, and you don't get the rolls. Frustration becomes your primary emotion as you beat yourself up over how poorly your skills are being demonstrated. Everything is on the bottom looking up.

No one is exempt from these experiences. The height and depth of the cycle can only be reduced through significant improvements in skills and knowledge. Proper training can help reduce the length of time on the down cycle, and extend the up cycle, but only by small amounts.

The key to surviving a down cycle is to identify when it starts. This is usually evident when you miss a couple of shots that should be within your comfort zone. With this warning, immediately reduce your expectations of success. Re-size your comfort zone down to about half to two-thirds its regular size. For example, if you are pretty good with 6 foot shots, on down cycles expect to be successful only with 3-4 foot shots.

The down cycle will last however long it is going to last. The only possible predictor is to calculate how long your up cycle lasted. You'll be able to feel the change from down to up when you notice a slight rise in your confidence level. This is the point where you can trust a larger comfort zone and thereby return to your normal game patterns.

www.ingramcontent.com/pod-product-compliance
Lightning Source LLC
LaVergne TN
LVHW061217060426
835507LV00016B/1974